Retirement Spotlight

Michael Foguth

Table of Contents

Introduction

Why should you read this book?

Because the lessons it contains will enable you to make wise decisions as you approach retirement.

And why do I believe my advice will benefit you?

Because I retire 200 times every year.

Even though I may not actually retire, I do walk alongside my clients as they retire. The effect is very similar: my clients share with me the experience of their hopes, dreams, and aspirations. Accompanying those are their fears, concerns, and anxieties.

For instance, I've worked through couples' health concerns. You may have the world's greatest plan, but what if God's plan is completely different? One couple I worked with wanted to prepare under the assumption that the husband would die first—usually a correct belief. They were afraid that if he died first his pension would vanish, leaving her with nothing. So we tried to plan to provide for the wife. We were initially unable to get the husband approved for life insurance, so we ended up insuring the wife first. Soon after that, she died prematurely and unexpectedly.

We can put a fantastic retirement plan together. But the plan here must understand that at the end of the day, God's plan counts the most. We are just here for a short period of time. That realization should spur us on to plan wisely— not arrogantly, but wisely.

You only get to retire once. And as soon as you have retired, you cannot retrace your steps and undo decisions you made 10 years ago. Worse, mistakes accompany inexperience. If you start a new activity, whether bowling or woodcarving or retiring, you will make first-time mistakes. The difference with retiring is that you do not get a second chance. That makes learning from others' experience all the more important. As author Roy H. Williams once said:

A smart man makes a mistake, learns from it, and never makes that mistake again. But a wise man finds a smart man and learns from him how to avoid the mistake altogether.

Remember the birth of your first child? You had no idea what to expect. Maybe you prepared thoroughly: attending classes, reading books. Hopefully that gave you some idea of what the experience would be like. But at the end of the day, I'll bet the most helpful advice came from some close friends—friends *who had already experienced what you were anticipating.*

I serve as a channel of retirement experience, from older retirees to you. Basing your expectations of retirement on someone else's real-life experience can be calming. It can set your mind at ease, giving you permission to reject fear and believe things will be okay. You are almost ready to retire—and that's thrilling.

That's why I retire 200 times a year: for you. I want to facilitate your retirement transition. I want you to enjoy every day of retirement, and go to bed peacefully for the rest of your life. It bothers me to see people overwhelmed and consumed by the financial aspect of retirement. That is extremely important, and I don't want to devalue it. But finances are truly not the most important element.

The goal of financial planning is life: full, free, joy-filled life. Money should not control who you are and what you do. I have no crystal ball, and my market predictions are not better than all other advisors' picks. But it's not about market predictions, or who dies with the largest number next to their name. The true point is *how you lived your life*. Did you do what you most wanted? Or did the market and your advisor hinder you from living to the full?

Many of those who walk through my door are already near their ideal life. They have worked hard for decades, and right now their money is supporting their desires. I passionately desire to see these people continue doing what is important to them, and not have to worry about the money day in and day out.

Others have assets, but haven't figured out how to employ them. I want to help them think through their ideal life, then work to get them there.

This book is titled *Retirement Spotlight* because I want to shine a spotlight on the topics retirees and pre-retirees commonly face. I'll expose myths and highlight reality. A spotlight both illuminates and reveals, and those two actions correspond to the two sections of this book.

- Section I. Illuminating Life – What is your ideal life?
- Section II. Revealing Finances – How do you reach that life?

The goal of this book is to get you to the point in retirement where you can continue engaging in the meaningful activities you enjoy. So the first half of this book focuses on the ideal life.

And the second half addresses the finances you need to get there.

In retirement, income is king. Without income you have no retirement. I practice *income-focused retirement planning*, which means I specialize in wielding your assets in a way intended to produce a steady and reliable income for you. You tell me what you want to accomplish. My job is to do all the real work and heavy lifting. I'll take the least amount of money possible and strive toward the maximum possible result.

For that reason, the book you are reading is not a do-it-yourself guide to retirement. Trust me— you don't want to do it yourself. Rather, this book is *educational*. Primarily I want you to learn the right questions to ask your advisor. Questions like:

- Will you put me in control of my income?
- Will I be able to change my benefits?

- What guaranteed income will you provide me?[1]

I am not going to spend a lot of time on buy-ins, caps, participation, and other nuts-and-bolts details. Your financial advisor can handle those competently—*if* you choose the right advisor.

A lot of advisors talk above their clients. They know a lot more about financial matters than their clients, so they (consciously or unconsciously) speak in terms their clients find hard to understand. Learning the right questions empowers you to bypass finance-speak and cut straight to the heart of the matter.

For instance, here's another great question. Perhaps your spouse asks you, "Hey honey— how much income are we guaranteed for next month?" If you don't know, you had better call

---

[1] Guaranteed income is based upon the financial strength of the issuing company as well as compliance with product requirements.

your advisor up right away. And if he can't tell you quickly, you need a new advisor.

Traditional retirement planning will always fail to give you a straight answer. In this style of planning you have a pension and Social Security, plus whatever withdrawals you take off of your investments. But that's the problem: if the withdrawal changes, your life changes. That puts your life at the whim of the markets.

In chapter seven I'll tell you a story about my grandma. She wasn't in control. Someone else controlled what she was going to do with the rest of her retirement. And that worked out, as long as the market was up. She could live her dream retirement. But as soon as the market got dicey, she and a lot of other retirees had to alter their standard of living. The market changed, and forced them to change along with it. That's no way to live.

One of my clients is a doctor. He told me that when the market crashed in 2008, he started working six days a week instead of five. Every time he lost money in his portfolio, he wanted to earn it back by working more hours.

It became a vicious cycle. His accounts kept decreasing, and his hours kept increasing. Instead of working eight hours a day, he started working twelve. Then sixteen. And then he went from six days a week to seven days a week.

He went on like this for nine months more, working seven days a week for 12-16 hours a day. But every time he opened up his statement, he was down more money. He was putting more in than ever before, but it kept leaking out.

Maybe you've experienced that too. Well, the second half of this book will educate you so you can choose the right financial advisor. Namely, an advisor who will never let that happen to you again.

And it's not just you who needs to be asking questions. An advisor worth his salt will ask you a heap of questions too. I can't tell you how many people meet with me and then say, "The advisor I've been with for fifteen years has never asked me that question." It just blows my mind.

For instance: Has your advisor asked you recently about your kids and grandkids? How often do you want to visit? Do you need to plan for an upcoming wedding? Are you going to save up out of your own money, or are you going to take a withdrawal?

If the market crashes ten percent, odds are you're not going out to California for that wedding. You won't spend a couple thousand dollars to make the trip. And if you do, you'll probably doubt your decision later and feel guilty.

Those are the uncertainties you want to get rid of. Identify the cardinal matters that keep you up at night, and get answers for them. Because too often people don't bring them up to their advisor—or their advisor doesn't bring the matters up to them—until it's too late. Monday morning, their advisor walks into the office and finds his voicemail light blinking: "Hey, the doctor unexpectedly told me that my spouse needs to go to a nursing home. I've got to come in and figure something out." Trying to plan after the fact cuts your options down from a hundred to two. Your advisor should be asking you preventative questions months ahead of time.

Or perhaps, "Hey, my husband Jack passed away unexpectedly over the weekend. Who is the beneficiary of all his money?" Once someone dies, you cannot change the beneficiary. I could tell you horror story after horror story. Many people set up their IRA or 401k with their wife alone as the beneficiary. What about the kids? What if both spouses die at the same time? What if she predeceases you, and then you die? Where does the money go? An advisor who is actually looking at your whole picture will ask those questions. Then he'll work on the answers for you.

You must be educated to choose an advisor who listens to your questions, and responds with good questions of his own. You can trust that advisor to make good decisions for you.

Educating you to find that perfect advisor is what this book is all about.

Section I. Illuminating Life

The Goal

Chapter 1. The Retiree's Transition

This chapter is for pre-retirees who wonder what life will look like after retirement. It's easy to make assumptions about retirement that are actually untrue. So in this chapter, we'll look at three myths you need to watch out for.

Myth #1: Retirement means sitting on the front porch swing with a book.

Retirement is active. It's seeing family, taking trips, playing golf. I know a guy who is eighty years old, and he still plays golf four times a week. What are your hobbies? Maybe you love reading or gardening. What have you always wanted to do, but never had time for? Retirement is when those longings flourish.

The financial aspect of retirement matters insofar as it affects your ideal life. If you like to drive down from Michigan to Florida for a few months every winter, you will need more driving days as you get older. You made it there in two days as a 50-year-old, and now at 75 you need a week. But if your financial life is in order, you can start taking an airplane instead.

What is it that you like to do? Odds are, you're going to continue to do it until you run out of money or you die. The myth is that retirement means you're going to stop doing what you love to do.

For some people, what they love to do is work. Maybe they don't want to work 40 (or 60) hours a week anymore. But they find meaning and fulfillment in their work, and aren't ready to close up shop just yet. They are at their highest earning potential, with stronger business relationships than ever before. More opportunities are available, and retirement may mean taking one of those opportunities.

Recently I met with someone who is retiring next January. He is going to transition from full-time work to part-time consulting. Later on he will become fully retired. He's looking at a few opportunities, from a six-month contract to a ten-month contract. Lifelong white-collar workers like him are highly sought after. Unlike a blue-collar worker whose productivity typically decreases as he ages, a white-collar worker gains more experience and skill the longer he works. Partial-retirement setups like this are a win-win situation. The retiree's transition is eased, and the business benefits from his work experience.

Ceasing to work a full-time job does not have to mean total inactivity. Instead, it may mean working for a time with an old friend in his business. Younger demographics take a job for six months, then move somewhere else for two years, then switch positions yet again. That's not unusual. But for someone in their 70s, working for more than two or three businesses over a lifetime would have been very strange. They met many different businesspeople; however, they only got to work with a few. When these friends hear that retirement is approaching, they want to create a business arrangement and finally get to work together. I see that very often.

Myth #2: We will spend less money in retirement.

Your retirement will include more than sitting on the porch with a book. The impact is that you will spend more money than ever before. Think about it: You are likely not going to wake up every day, make eggs for breakfast, read the newspaper, have a turkey sandwich for lunch, putter around the house, eat another turkey sandwich for dinner, go to bed, and repeat. You are going to be active! You will go to restaurants with your friends. You'll run to Home Depot and pick up the supplies you need to finally finish your Honey-Do projects around the house. You will re-landscape your yard, create a garden, remodel your workshop. Whatever you love to do, retirement frees you to do more of it.

As a current pre-retiree, on which day of the week do you spend the most money? Tuesday?

I bet not. You spend the most money on the weekend. And retirement is an everlasting weekend, with six Saturdays and one Sunday. The pace of the new extended weekend changes—you aren't rushed, with only one day to pack activities into. But the costs of the weekend remain.

You should especially budget more money for the first 12 months after retirement. Reward yourself for working hard over the decades. You made it! A lot of people reach the retirement finish line and fail to realize they won the race. You are fortunate to have accomplished a goal that many people never do.

Embrace the initial rush of retirement. Take a victory lap after your race. On the days you hated the office most, what kept you going? What made you think, "I cannot wait to do [that], so I will keep plugging now"? You could hardly wait. So now go and live you dream.

Myth #3: The pace of life will slow down in retirement.

The popular image of retirement includes lazy days, with all the time in the world, and not much happening.

For most people, that is an inaccurate impression of retirement. One of my clients is trying to adjust to the "new normal" of retirement, but struggling because it doesn't feel like the new normal. It feels like the old normal, with life speeding up instead of slowing down. He is trying to establish a non-work-related identity, but it's not what he expected.

"Who am I?" is a surprisingly frequent question in retirement. After working for decades, people have to find a new core for their identity. They've always been able to walk up to anyone, shake their hand, and introduce themselves as "Bob Smith, purchasing director for General Motors." Their identity was tied up with their company. Now how do they introduce themselves? "Bob Smith, retired purchasing director"? Nobody does that. So one is left with "Bob Smith" and has to recreate the sense of identity.

There may initially be a mismatch between your retirement expectations and retirement reality. The accompanying need is to reestablish your identity on something other than the job you took. You are not going to transform into a radically different person in retirement. Your job may be no more, but the person you are beneath the exterior is unchanged. You just need something else to do: a new passion.

Who are you now? Work was your calling for the past decades. Now something new and better will take its place.

Chapter 2. The Retiree's Activities

As you approach retirement, you need to ask yourself two important questions about your activities. First, What do you want to do? And second, How long do you want to do it? Let's look at each of these in turn.

Question #1. *What* do you want to do?

Sit down and really think about what you want to do. Imagine your retirement: time is on your side. You don't have to do go work. You don't have to do anything. What do you want to do in the next five years? The next five months? You have big goals and small goals, and retirement holds enough time to accomplish them all.

Some goals you can reach in five months. Others you can't. If you really want to tour Europe, we might not be able to swing that financially in the next five months. But if you plan it for the next five years? With the right plan we might be able to get you there in two.

"I want to travel" is a really common answer. It's a good one, and you should plan a trip if you want to see the world. Keep in mind, though, that if you haven't been a traveler for your entire life you may not become one in retirement. Take the Alaskan cruise, sure. But do you really want to be on the road and in hotels all the time? Maybe you do. Maybe you don't.

Perhaps the traveling you want to do is focused less on *places* and more on *people*. Say you live in Michigan and your favorite granddaughter is getting married in California. You want to be able to fly to California, stay in a hotel for a few nights, and see the sights with your family.

My clients talk a lot about family. They want to go see their grandkids graduate. Or they have four grandchildren of marriageable age, so they need to save up for a lot of trips.

Retirement should be full of meaningful activities. Don't forget that these meaningful activities can be centered around others! Engage in activities with a purpose.

Question #2. *How long* do you want to do it?

We're living longer than ever before. The U.S. life expectancy at birth in the year 1930 was only 60 years. Someone born here today is expected to live over 79 years.[2]

Factors such as infant mortality lower those numbers, though—the outlook for pre-retirees is even sunnier. According to the Social Security Administration:

> *"A man reaching age 65 today*
> *can expect to live, on average,*
> *until age 84.3.*

---

[2] *Life Expectancy*, Centers for Disease Control and Prevention, June 13, 2016, available at http://www.cdc.gov/nchs/fastats/life-expectancy.htm. A hard copy is available upon request by contacting our office: 810-522-5650 or Michael@FoguthFinancial.com.

A woman turning age 65 today
can expect to live, on average,
until age 86.6.

And those are just averages.
About one out of every four
65-year-olds today will live
past age 90, and one out of 10
will live past age 95."[3]

If you search for "life expectancy calculator" on the Social Security Administration website (ssa.gov), you can find your current life expectancy based on your birthdate. You might be surprised.

If you have a one in four chance of living past age 90, then you need to financially plan well into your 90s. And you may be doing much

---

[3] *Calculators: Life Expectancy*, Social Security Administration, available at https://www.ssa .gov/planners/lifeexpectancy.html. A hard copy is available upon request by contacting our office: 810-522-5650 or Michael@FoguthFinancial.com.

more than sitting in a rocking chair. Sure, you may not travel Asia. But might you want to travel to a wedding? My clients Bob and Dot retired 20 years ago. In theirs 80s, they are still doing many of the same activities as in their 60s. The intensity is lower, but the frequency is not. Attending graduations and family reunions is a regular part of their schedule. Because they planned properly years ago, they have not been forced to slow down.

This is called *continued mobility.* Plan today as if you'll be engaging in the same activities 20 years down the road. What if you want to take a relaxing cruise at age 85? Maybe that won't be possible. But maybe it will be. Don't make a bad decision at 65 that prevents you from living your dream at 85.

Your lifestyle substantially impacts on your continued mobility. If you make health a priority in retirement, you are likely to live longer and more actively. Many of my clients have wanted to focus on their health for many years, but always been sidetracked by work.

Retirement is their opportunity! Or to put it negatively, now they have no excuse. Join the gym! Learn how to cook food that is both nutritious and delicious. Find an exercise routine you actually enjoy. Aided by advances in medical technology, your investment in your own health will pay major dividends.

Consider what you want to do in retirement. Then realize how long you need to plan for. But no matter how long you live, at some point you will have to leave your family. What legacy do you want to stay behind for those you love? That's the topic of the next chapter.

Chapter 3. The Retiree's Legacy

What legacy do you desire to leave to your family?

I have no desire to be morbid, but one day we are all going to die. Living in light of the last day should bring clarity to this day. How do you want to be remembered? Okay. What action must you take today to accomplish that?

I believe there are two main types of legacies: financial and personal. You want to leave both. Let's take a closer look, starting with your financial legacy.

Part 1: Financial Legacy

As I write this, I had a client meeting earlier today with a man who is on pace to leave $1.6 million to his two daughters. We ran the appropriate calculations based on the amount of income they would take each month. Everything looked good. His financial legacy to them would significantly contribute to their wellbeing. Then we took a step back. I asked him, "How would you react if I told you that this $1.6 million is going to be worth closer to $300,000 in twenty years?" There was a long silence. I don't think it really registered. In terms of buying power, $1.6 million *then* won't be worth much more than $300,000 *today*.

One impact is that you should not be concerned that you are giving too much money to your descendants. In reality, some retirees would like to give much more—but they don't want to lose control of their money.

Thankfully, it is possible to build a legacy plan without losing control of your money. Without delving into exact scenarios, I will say that you can buy certain forms of life insurance and then get back all the premiums you paid in if you change your mind. Call my office and set up an appointment with me if you want to know more.

Other clients walk into my office and tell me their philosophy is, "What's left is left." They have poured their lives into their children and don't feel obligated to leave them a large amount of money. And I very much respect that mentality. I explain to them that legacy planning is not about removing money from their pockets so it can pad their children's pockets later on. Instead, the purpose of legacy planning is to use all your money well, both now and later.

If they spend it all while they are still alive, more power to them. But if some is left over, I bet they would prefer it to be more rather than less. They have worked long and hard for their money—now is the time to make that money work long and hard for them. If they don't use it, I would rather see extra funds go to their children and grandchildren than vanish because of poor planning.

Part 2: Personal Legacy

Alongside your financial legacy, you want to leave a personal one. This is perhaps epitomized by the saying, "I want to see them smile when they get the check—not just cash it when I'm gone." As thankful as your family may be for your financial legacy, they can only say Thank You while you're still around. Maximize your memories now.

My grandma never missed a single one of my childhood baseball games. And I was always glad to see her. But it wasn't until I got older that I realized what a commitment she made. It was a commitment of money to buy fuel for the car and post-game treats for me; it was a commitment of time to spend those hours watching me every single week. Her sacrifice made an indelible imprint on me.

Clients have told me they want to help their kids out with student loan or house debt. A lot of my clients help their grandkids with tuition, at the private school or college level. Or they help them buy their first cars. Leaving a personal legacy means you get to see the good effects of your generosity. One of my clients planned a great family trip, and 15 years later everyone in the family is still talking about it.

Now, you have to be careful here. You don't want to spend all your money on somebody else and leave yourself in trouble. Living longer than ever before (as mentioned above) complicates this further. The solution is to maximize your income early on. You can set up your retirement plan such that you are guaranteed[4] a set amount of income every single month for the rest of your life. As a result, you have more than enough income arriving regularly. Don't think you need millions and millions of dollars. You just need to maximize whatever amount you have.

To sum all this legacy planning up, my personal philosophy on the matter is two simple words:

---

[4] Guarantees are based on the financial strength of the issuer as well as compliance with product requirements.

Others First. That's how I look at things. I am willing to make personal sacrifices to increase the happiness of someone I love and hold dear.

I'm willing to sacrifice to be on the field. I coach my kids in all their sports, Monday–Wednesday–Saturday: probably six hours a week. Not to mention staying up until 2:00 a.m. with my wife, sending out emails to the team. Those sorts of things don't cost money, but are personally impactful.

Even if you do invest heavily in your children and grandchildren, you may be taken for granted. At least, until that kid grows up and finds it's their turn. Then they look back and say, "Wow! My mom and dad (or grandma and grandpa) made a lot of sacrifices. Because I know what I'm doing right now is not easy!"

Let me share two quotes that I find motivating. Here's the first:

Make a short-term sacrifice
for a long-term gain.

That's not a financial saying; it's a life saying. Deciding to sacrifice for another is hard. But remember that you are investing for the long term. One day your kids will get the chance to be parents, to experience everything you have experienced. All your hard work will pay off that day. Short-term sacrifice, long-term gain. Here's the second saying:

If it were easy,
everybody would do it.

I don't want to say that leaving a legacy is easy, as if you wake up one day and find that everything is set up for you. It's going to take some work. And it doesn't necessarily have to be financial work. Sometimes your presence means more to your family than a check ever could.

Maybe your grandson's birthday is coming up. You could mail him a card and a check for $100, and he would be grateful. Or you could plan a trip, drive to wherever he lives, and spend a few days with the family. If they are out of state, it may cost you $500 to travel and $300 for the hotel. That's an $800 birthday gift. When your grandson opens the card—which now has a $20 check inside—he may not realize that. But when he grows up, you bet he will. He'll remember your $800 investment in him.

That story illustrates how money isn't the point, in and of itself. Mailing a $100 check is not as impactful as a personal visit. But money still has to play a role: if you are going to travel to your grandchildren on their birthdays, you need money to spend on fuel and hotels. The personal investment requires more money than the merely financial investment, which would cost a grand total of $100.49 (counting the stamp).

I find most people identify with that story. They don't want their retirement to be totally about them and their money. They want their retirement to count, in creating experiences and leaving behind good memories. They value family.

I was taught to value family by sheer volume of exposure. My mother and my father were both members of large families, and everyone on my mother's side basically lived in the same community. Every month at least one person had a birthday, so we would all get together and celebrate. We would go to someone's house, have dinner, eat cake, and spend lots of time together. All my cousins and I would have a blast.

On my father's side, get-togethers were less frequent but just as large. Every time we came together for Christmas, a wedding, a graduation, or a funeral, at least 70 people showed up. Larger families mean more life events, and I was continually surrounded by family. Everyone made it a point to come.

That's where my Others First mentality comes from. Would it have been easier and cheaper not to attend the wedding of the cousin who lived in Wisconsin? Sure! We lived in Michigan. We could have avoided making plans, booking hotels, packing the car, and traveling. Not going is much easier. But we went, even when it was a sacrifice. That's how I learned the value of family and putting others first.

Earlier I told you that I coach all my kids' sporting activities. Well, my father coached me and my siblings at every activity we did growing up. For traveling sports teams, he would take off with us right after work ended, having reserved hotel rooms for Friday and Saturday night. It wasn't cheap. Growing up I never realized this, because I didn't have the responsibility. But now I look back and say, "Wow, they put me first." It makes me want to do the same to others.

In order to put others first in retirement, you have to plan right. Otherwise you will put your family first until you're 80, then realize that you're broke. But if you have a proper plan set up, you can sleep well at night and not worry about going broke.

In Section II we'll explore this idea. You'll learn to choose a financial advisor who can set up the right income plan for you, empowering you to live your retirement dream.

Section II. Revealing Finances

The Process

Chapter 4. The Retiree's Identity

This second section is about how you can reach the goal we outlined in Section I. You want to attain this ideal retirement: continue doing things that are important to you, start doing new things you never had the opportunity for, create memories with your family. How do you get there?

You have to look at the financial aspect. That starts with how you—your identity and goals— affect your finances. And it concludes with how your finances affect you.

Who are you? And who will you become in retirement? Perhaps surprisingly, you'll be the same person you've always been. Retirement is not going to change your essence. Surface details will change—but the *you* underneath will not.

Too many people anticipate restrictions of mind, body, and interest in retirement. I have sat and listened to very outgoing people tell me, "I'm preparing to be alone a lot more in retirement. My mind isn't going to last, so I'll have to be less social." How awful! An outgoing person now will stay outgoing in retirement. As the years pass they may mellow, but dramatic decrease is unlikely.

Don't let the second phase of your life differ dramatically from the first. Here's a helpful thought exercise: consider your life thus far, and identify what you have most enjoyed. Plan the second phase around those enjoyments. If you're going to change in retirement, then make sure it's your choice. The key word there is *your*. Your choice. Not the market's choice. Not someone else's choice. Your goal is to change not because of external forces, but only because of your own internal decisions.

Thus far we've talked about your identity in terms of personality. But another aspect of identity is your nature. Your retirement expectations must be informed by every element of who you are, DNA in addition to disposition.

Let's consider your generational history, the source of both sober realities and unexpected joys. The sober reality is that you cannot escape your family lineage. Today I met with a couple who told me the husband's oldest living family member is 67. In contrast, the wife's oldest living family member is in her 90s. Being both in their 60s, this couple is very concerned about how generational history may affect their retirement. They need to plan to provide for the wife in case the husband predeceases her.

That's the dark cloud of generational history. But every cloud has a silver lining—sometimes a substantial one. Happily, that's the case here.

The term "generational gap" is used to refer to a difference of opinions between older and younger generations. But I like to use it with an additional meaning: a difference of *outcome* between generations.

Think of it this way. Your dad and mom lived in an era with certain possibilities. They had access to a level of medical care, a level of nutritional information, a level of exercise routines. A few decades later, you have access to a vastly increased array of possibilities. You can use those possibilities to create a gap in your generational line.

Take medical technology. Breakthrough advances in just the past 15 years include mapping the human genome, targeted cancer therapies, minimally invasive surgeries, and bionic limbs.[5]

Aside from such technology, you have a role to play too. Take practical action: visit the doctor for a physical twice a year instead of once. Work to prevent the diseases you are prone to

---

[5] *10 Medical Advances in the Last 10* Years, CNN, June 5, 2013, available at http://www.cnn.com/2013/06/05/health/lifeswork-medical-advances/. A hard copy is available upon request by contacting our office: 810-522-5650 or Michael@FoguthFinancial.com.

because of family history. Eat deliciously and nutritiously (it can be done!). Let medical technology work in your favor, and complement it with your own daily lifestyle.

Too often I hear people say, "My folks never did that" as a reason to dismiss a new possibility. Maybe they didn't. But maybe they *would have*, if they'd had access to the advances you do. Just because something is new doesn't make it inferior to the tried and true. Someday these newfangled possibilities will be the new standard. So break open a generational gap. Plan ahead. Commit to live fully, with all the aid this world can give you.

If you watch TV news, you regularly see stories of 100-year-olds doing incredible things. They don't merely sit in nursing homes and pass the time away. They run marathons, write books, waterski, continue their education, climb mountains, and more. What will you do?

People who live to be a hundred years old may accumulate quite a few wrinkles. Their hair may be white. But nobody says their mind has to be gone. The potentials and possibilities of old age are always increasing.

You never know when your time will be up. Even if you plan for 100, live every year as though it could be your last. Maybe you hear all this good news and think, "I might live to 100! That means I can't do anything now. I need to reserve all my capital for later." That's not the right response. If God calls your number at 76, you don't want to regret the past decade because you were hoping for two more. Find an advisor who can build a plan for living to 100 without personal and financial sacrifices.

You want to live life to the full today. Your life expectancy may be short or long, and your actual life may differ from your life expectancy. Regardless: you need to be ready today, living without regrets and full of joy.

Chapter 5. The Retiree's Goals

The dual goals for your retirement income plan are safety and growth. Safety, because there are no do-overs in retirement. You can't go back and say, "I will do that differently the second time around." Hindsight is 20/20, but that does you no good. You can't avoid the 2008 financial crises now that we're years past it.

The most important kind of safety is safety of *income*, not safety of *assets*. That is a significant distinction. Income is always the priority in retirement, though safety of assets is also very important. See, people retire because they have enough income to retire. They have a pension and Social Security—guaranteed streams of income. However, sometimes those two alone are not enough. That's where the third stream of personal savings comes in. The three streams should be put together into a retirement income plan that guarantees you a set income for life.

One implication is that the conception of "finding your retirement number" is flawed. Sometimes you hear well-meaning financial advisors say, "You need to reach a million dollars [or two million] in your retirement account. Then you'll be set." This approach is flawed because it focuses on assets, and doesn't adequately address your income needs in retirement.

Income safety obviously comes before income growth. But growth, the second goal, is vital too. As you move through retirement, you need to give yourself regular pay raises. Why? Because cost of goods is more today than it was 25 years ago. And it will be still more in another 25 years.

In 1990, a postage stamp cost 25¢. A loaf of bread was $1.29. Gas was $1.08 per gallon. A new car cost about $9,400. And the average income was under $15,000. Inflation makes a difference. So when you are planning for your retirement, you have to make sure you have increases in your retirement income.[6]

We'll talk more about safety in chapters 6-7, then turn to growth in chapter 8.

---

[6] *Prices in the 90s*, In the 90s, available at http://www.inthe90s.com/prices.shtml. A hard copy is available upon request by contacting our office: 810-522-5650 or Michael@FoguthFinancial.com.

Chapter 6. The Retiree's Control

Are you in control of your retirement income?

You might say, "Of course!" But are you really? The three streams of retirement income are pension, Social Security, and personal savings. Let's look at each and see how much control you truly have.

We'll start with Social Security. In retirement, you will receive a Social Security check from the government. You're not really in control. It is what it is. More importantly, with the deficit, Social Security may experience changes that have the potential to impact you negatively. However, studies indicate that if you are over the age of 55, you will not see too many negative impacts to your Social Security. The implication? If you are under 55, you really need to be concerned.

The government may not publicly say, "We are taking money out of retirees' Social Security accounts." But they may still pay you differently. How so? Well, how will your Social Security income be taxed? They might give you the same amount of money—but if tax rates increase, you are receiving less. Government likes to get its way through the back door, instead of publicly using the front door. As long as they get their revenue, they're happy to use backhanded accounting tricks and leave you in the dark.

If the government keeps your Social Security check the same amount but increases taxes by 10%, you just took a 10% hit. You now net 10% less money than you did last year, but you are paying for the same amount of income. A tax increase would have the same effect as a governmental withdrawal from your Social Security account—but it would come in the form of your April tax return. You have to be careful with Social Security. You're not in control there.

If the government does decide to raise taxes or take other negative action, you want to be prepared. How can you position your assets and your income so they don't get hit incredibly hard?

The best thing you can do is position your assets as tax-free payouts. For a retiree, the most common vehicle is a Roth IRA. So much needs to be said about the value of tax-free payouts that I've decided to write an entire book about it. This is a huge opportunity for retirees, so my next book will be about how to convert your assets from taxable to tax-free.

If you want a preview before the next book comes out, check out my website, www.FoguthFinancial.com. You can get access to a helpful retirement kit, including three guides that address topics you should consider when planning your retirement. One of those guides is on this very issue of tax-free money and Roth IRAs. Check it out!

Are you in control of your pension? Company pensions are big here in the Midwest. The three big automotive companies have them, along with many others. The problem with many pensions is that when they were first set up, they were "priced long." That is, the founders didn't think people would live as long as they do today. Combine that with investments underperforming, and the pension funds don't contain as much money as anticipated.

Because of this, the companies have had to come out and make some pretty dramatic changes. You are not going to get the exact same amount you thought, and there's nothing you can do about it. The company is in control of that paycheck—just as the government can control your Social Security. Like the government can mess with the taxes on your Social Security income, a pension company can mess with your pension. For instance, they'll get rid of your health benefits. So now you have to pay those out-of-pocket, rather than your pension supplementing them.

What practical steps can you take to regain control of your retirement? It all starts with safe investments, which we'll address in the next chapter.

Chapter 7. The Retiree's Guarantee

In retirement, you receive your income through a pension and through Social Security. But you can also create your own stream of income—one you can control. In this chapter we'll evaluate what this looks like in practice.

You want a stream of income that is safe. Now, we need to distinguish between *safe* money and *safer* money. Safer money is not always safe. Too often "safer" means "less risk"—but any risk at all is not safe. Whether you have more risk or less risk, you still have the potential to lose it all.

People think they are better off financially because they have moved their money into bonds or less-risky investments. In reality, they still hold risk. Losing value on that investment is entirely plausible. Therefore, "safer" investments do not provide a safe income stream; there is no guarantee you will be able to draw from it every single year for the rest of your life.

This is especially true in retirement. Most financial advisors counsel retirees to keep their money in safer investments. However, a retiree who loses only 10% (instead of the 20% riskier investors lost) is still in a bad place. Don't be fooled by terminology: safer money and safe money are not the same.

As you strive to gain control over an increasing percentage of your retirement income, you want to guarantee that income. Because in the end, the key is not how much money you have. The key is how much income you can sustainably draw. As long as you are employed, you have a guaranteed stream of income. Your bank account might be low (especially when you are young); however, that stream of income from your employment keeps you afloat. As soon as you retire, you have to recreate that guaranteed income stream.

This is what my clients want from their income plan: an income they cannot outlive, guaranteed regardless of downturns, allowing them freedom to do what they desire. Of course, all guaranteed income depends on the financial strength of the issuer as well as your compliance with the terms of the product.

Guaranteed retirement income should be your number one priority. You must be able to go to bed tonight and know that when you wake up tomorrow, your income will still be there. And it will be there when you wake up next month, and in ten months, and in ten years. Contractually guarantee yourself enough income to secure the absolute minimum of what you want to do.

I address these ideas more in a free video series on my website, www.FoguthFinancial.com. If you'd like to dig in further go check it out—the videos are part of the "Helpful Retirement Kit."

Here's another terminology distinction: when discussing income streams, the goal is not *return* but *payout.* The difference is critical. *Return* refers to the increase of the asset itself: If you put $1,000 in an asset with a return of 5%, you will soon have $1,050. *Payout* refers to the level of income that asset provides you. Perhaps the asset only grows in value from $1,000 to $1,001; but if it guarantees you an income of $50, that's a smart investment.

Your retirement planning focus should be level of payout, not rate of return. Don't worry overly much about the increase of the asset itself. Be concerned about the level of guaranteed income it can promise you.

Imagine this scenario: you're offered the choice of two assets. Both offer you the level of monthly income you need. The first asset guarantees a 4% rate of return, but no more. The second asset has no guarantee, but has been trending at a 7% rate of return. Which would you choose?

Many people would choose Asset #2. After all, the return is 3% greater! But consider this. Why would you risk everything for that extra 3%? Sure, 7% is great—but if you only need the level of monthly income that 4% will provide, why take on the risk?

Murphy's Law applies to investing. Anything that can go wrong, will go wrong...eventually. That 7% asset may skyrocket for a few years. But just as you're preparing for your 50th wedding anniversary trip, the stock market dips and your asset loses half of its value. You were getting ready to go on the vacation of your dreams, and now you have to sell off assets at a loss to fund the trip. That's the last thing you want to do.

Unfortunately, I speak on these matters from first-hand family experience. Near the turn of the millennium, my grandma retired from the family automotive supply business. She could finally do what she had waited her whole life to do. She went out to breakfast every morning instead of cooking; she travelled throughout the country visiting family and friends. But then the 2001-2002 recession hit, and her portfolio did a flip-flop. Her finances weakened, and she had to make lifestyle changes. She could no longer do everything she wanted to do.

Because her assets took a big dip, she could no longer feel comfortable spending what remained on luxury items.

By "luxury" I don't mean extravagance. I mean everything above a basic standard of living: eating out, going to the movies, buying a new shirt just because you like it. If you have a steady stream of income during retirement, you can feel free to go out to eat instead of fixing your own breakfast. You are afforded the luxuries and finer things in life. You are confident that if you spend the money today, it's going to be there again tomorrow—and the next month, and the next year. As soon as that confidence disappears and your safety net is yanked out from underneath you, you cut back and stop those things.

Similarly, during the 2008 recession I saw people with second homes selling them at a loss. Why? Because when finances are tight, luxuries have to go. These people realized they had to tighten their belts, so they took a hard look at things: "What do we absolutely have to have? Well, we don't have to have a second home. We don't have to have a third vehicle. We don't have to go on the Caribbean cruise. We don't have to go and visit the family this year. It'd be nice to have and do them, but we could skip them." This is the dark underside of high-risk 7% return assets: sometimes they yield negative 7% instead. And then you are forced to change your lifestyle.

As we consider the main financial vehicles—stocks, bonds, mutual funds, CDs, and annuities—we realize that only one is guaranteed. An annuity is the only financial vehicle that can absolutely, contractually guarantee you an income you cannot outlive. Those guarantees are based solely upon the claims-paying ability of the issuing company as well as compliance with the annuity product's requirements.

By definition, an annuity is a stream of income you cannot outlive. For instance, your rich uncle could leave you an annuity of $1,000 in his will. That means you would receive $1,000 every year for the rest of your life. Financial annuities are a bit more complex, but work the same fundamental way.

If you want to talk about the specifics of annuities, give my office a call at 810-522-5650 or 866-854-4149. I'd be happy to explain the details further.

Annuities also provide protection for the surviving spouse in case of premature death. An unexpectedly early death can negatively affect both your pension and Social Security payouts.

For Social Security, if you die your spouse gets to keep the greater of your two payouts. For instance, if the husband receives $2,000 per month and the wife receives $1,000 a month, at the death of either spouse only the $2,000 payout remains. The other is no longer available.

Your pension is a bit more complicated. Before they retire, each employee chooses what they would like their spouse to receive upon their passing. This decision affects the retirement income payout. When the employees retire, the amount of monthly income they receive is based partly on how much they want to leave their spouse. Three common payout options exist:

- Life Only. This monthly payment will be the highest, but it will only be paid out for the life of the retiree.
- Fifty Percent. This monthly payment will be somewhat lower. In this scheme, upon the pension holder's death the surviving spouse receives fifty percent of the original monthly payout. If the husband is receiving $2,000 monthly from his pension, when he dies his wife continues to receive $1,000 monthly for the rest of her life.
- Joint Life. This monthly payment will be the smallest. However, it will guarantee

the same amount to be paid out for both spouses' entire lives.

Your pension is actually a form of annuity. In this case, you receive the pension annuity from the company. The company owns the annuity and you are just a payee.

But you can essentially buy the exact same financial vehicle that your company buys for you at your retirement. If you purchase your own annuity, you can set it up to protect your spouse in case of premature death. The same three payout options as your pension will be available; you also have a few other options. You can elect to receive payouts for your life plus a certain number of years, perhaps 10. Or you can choose to have any remaining amount paid to your beneficiaries upon your death: if you invested $100,000 and the annuity had only paid out $50,000, the balance would go to your beneficiaries in a lump sum. These options are yours if you purchase an annuity of your own.

Chapter 8. The Retiree's Growth

The beauty of owning your own annuity is that you personalize it to yourself. You can decide that you want not only income, but also *growing* income. One of the payout options on an annuity will allow you to pick increasing income. Elect for this route, and the amount of money you receive each month will increase over time. The increasing option will start with a smaller payment and then grow over time, as opposed to a constant payment—which would start higher but stay stagnant.

Personalization is an important aspect of annuity planning. The difference between people means you're going to need different levels of income. How much income do you need? Everybody's going to be different. Some people are natural savers, and others are natural spenders. These are just a few considerations:

- Is your house paid off?
- Do you want to travel extensively?

- Is your family large, with lots of upcoming weddings and graduations?
- Do you want to remodel parts of your house?
- Are you going to re-landscape the yard?
- Do you want to vacation regularly?

Your answers to these questions and more affect the level of retirement income you need. Some of my clients want to take two grand trips every year. In contrast, I just had some clients come in and say, "We're simple people. We plan on watching our grandkids in retirement, and that's it. We have no desire to travel. We have no desire to go much of anywhere outside our town." Different people have diverse income needs, and you need to plan for that.

Anticipate life's curve balls too. Money-sucking surprising pop up all the time—even in retirement. And you'll likely spend more money in general, as we discussed in previous chapters. You are entering a season of endless weekends, and we all spend more money on the weekends. Prepare accordingly.

Chapter 9. The Retiree's Future

Retirement planning today is intended to secure your future. Three vital future considerations are long-term care, legacy planning, and estate planning. In this chapter we will discuss each in turn, hopefully beginning to point your thinking in the right direction.

Long-Term Care

Long-term care costs can catch you off guard. If you are married, here is the question you must ask: "How will one spouse's long-term care costs affect the other spouse?"

If you have no plan in place right now, you would most likely have to spend all of your household's money caring for the ill individual. Once the spouse needing care passes away, the surviving healthy spouse is left with no financial resources.

I wish there were a simple solution. But just like so many other aspects of retirement, it's complicated. Your situation is unique, and needs a personalized plan. Speak to your financial advisor and your estate planning attorney. Give my office a call at 810-522-5650 or 866-845-4149. Talk with an experienced professional who knows you and your needs, then work out a plan together.

You need to know what happens if either one of you gets sick. Where will the money come from to pay for it? The basic problem is that most states do not provide long-term care assistance until you have exhausted your own resources. This leaves the healthy spouse high and dry, with nothing to live off of.

You may be able to reposition some of your assets so they are exempt from this requirement. In that case, you could be assisted without having to impoverish yourself first. Each state has different laws, and you should consult a professional before making any decisions. The most important thing here is to know what would happen before it actually happens.

Legacy Planning

When you plan on leaving a legacy to your heirs, you want to maximize it. That's what legacy planning is all about.

This isn't essential for everyone. If you plan to spend most of your money while you're alive—on yourself or on your family—you may have no need for legacy planning. But if you expect to leave a substantial sum to your heirs, you'll want to ensure most of it actually goes to them and not to the IRS.

Aspects of legacy planning include life insurance, tax evaluation, and IRA conversion. You might want to turn your qualified investments (like IRAs) into nonqualified investments (like Roth IRAs) so your children can avoid taxation. Legacy planning involves choosing financial vehicles such that when you pass away, the money you have remaining truly reaches your kids.

Estate Planning

To put it colloquially, estate planning is making sure all your ducks are in a row. For instance, it includes checking that your beneficiaries are all updated: from beneficiaries of checking and savings accounts all the way up to beneficiaries of your financial vehicles.

Estate planning means arranging for your assets to be managed and distributed after your death. You want to have all the pieces of this asset-transfer puzzle in place, financially and otherwise. Who receives the house? Who gets the car? Which pieces of jewelry go to whom? Where does mom's wedding ring go? How are collectibles divided up? The more detail-oriented you can be here, the better off your estate plan will be.

If you don't plan your estate well enough, some of your assets may be awarded to the state upon your death. The state will send the case over to probate court, which will settle the account. Even if no one contests your heirs' claims in probate court, it's still a lot of time and money out the window. And in probate, your private information becomes public knowledge.

Estate planning should cause you to think of a million little things to take care of before you're gone. Some of my clients keep folders of all the bills they pay, so their heirs can pay or cancel them easily. In the end, someone will have to do the nitty-gritty detailed organization work. It's either going to be you now, or your dependents later—possibly through the courts. It's a whole lot more time and trouble than you intend to leave them. That's the wrong sort of legacy. Use estate planning to leave the best possible legacy instead.

Chapter 10. The Retiree's Advisor

What are your expectations of your financial advisor?

That's a crucial question. If your expectations do not match up with what an advisor offers, you are doomed to dissatisfaction.

What are you and your advisor trying to accomplish? Which financial race are you running: a sprint, or a marathon? Different monetary goals have various finish lines. Are you trying to make your money grow? Are you trying to make your money last? Are you trying to draw income from it?

Expectations are essential to satisfaction. If you have no expectations, how do you know what success looks like? If you don't have your expectations lined out so you know what they are, it's like running a race without a finish line at all. Or worse, you discover you're running the wrong race. You wanted your advisor to join you on a marathon of 26.2 miles, but he's running the 100-meter dash. He uses everything he has for that first 100 meters and looks great. But then he has nothing left in the tank.

Here are some areas of expectation you need to consider when evaluating a financial advisor.

#1. Loyalty

Is your advisor most concerned about you, or their company and the shareholders?

Most people expect their advisor to be primarily loyal to them. But that has not always been the case. Until recently, only a subset of financial advisors called *fiduciaries* were obligated to put their clients first. But within the past six months, the Department of Labor finalized a rule requiring all advisors to abide by this fiduciary standard. Here's an excerpt from the official summary:

> While many advisers do act in their customers' best interest, not everyone is legally obligated to do so and some do not. Many investment

professionals, consultants, brokers, insurance agents and other advisers operate within compensation structures that are misaligned with their customers' interests and often create strong incentives to steer customers into particular investment products.

[The new fiduciary rule] will protect investors by requiring all who provide retirement investment advice to plans, plan fiduciaries and IRAs to abide by a "fiduciary" standard— putting their clients' best interest before their own profits.[7]

This new rule turned on the lights for many people. They always thought their advisors were acting in their best interests, but now they

---

[7] *Fact Sheet: Department of Labor Finalizes Rule to Address Conflicts of Interest in Retirement Advice, Saving Middle Class Families Billions of Dollars Every Year*, U.S. Department of Labor, available at https://www.dol.gov/agencies/ebsa/about-ebsa/our-activities/resource-center/fact-sheets/dol-final-rule-to-address-conflicts-of-interest. A hard copy is available upon request by contacting our office: 810-522-5650 or Michael@FoguthFinancial.com.

realize they were deceived. Many advisors did not have their clients' wellbeing at heart. Their loyalty was to their company and its shareholders, not the retirees and pre-retirees they counseled. That revelation has been shocking to many people. Again, common sense seems to indicate that your advisor has to put your interests before his company's. But reality was the opposite.

The impacts of this new rule—which will come into effect in April 2017 and full effect in January 2018—are profound. Retirees with an advisor who was formerly not a fiduciary will now receive better service. But ironically, they may receive less of it.

Here's how that works. Under the new rule, the big-shot financial advisor can no longer charge what he used to. This means that the small guy on the block is going to be at a disadvantage. He is going to get less attention than he was formerly receiving—or no attention at all.

The Department of Labor's goal was to make every advisor a fiduciary for their clients. They accomplished that goal; however, the fear is that advisors who now feel limited in their earning potential will neglect smaller clients. They will think, "I could spend my time and energy on somebody else who has a bigger account." For simplicity's sake, let's say the new Department of Labor rule sets the percentage an advisor can earn at a flat 1%. If an advisor makes 1% on a five-million-dollar account, that's more money in his pocket than 1% on a one-million-dollar account. That is five times the earning for the exact same work. This provides a perverse incentive for the advisor to coddle the five-million-dollar client and ignore the little guy.

It's like a hotel chain that gets hit with the regulation that they have to put clean pillows in every single room. If they haven't been doing that before, they're going to start putting clean pillows in all the rooms—but they might raise the room rates. The really rich people who come stay at the hotel don't have any problem with that, but the little guy who just needs a place to sleep for the night and wants some good basic service is out in the cold.

The best idea is for you to go find an advisor who's been a fiduciary from the very beginning and isn't changing anything. The Department of Labor has vindicated him and his approach.

#2. Client-Centeredness

What is your first meeting with a potential advisor like? Watch out for "the grass is greener on the other side" language. Their sales pitch should not be focused around themselves, their products, and what they can do. They should pay attention to you and your unique needs. Are they focused on what they can do, or on what you *want* to do?

Your advisor needs to focus on you and your expectations in particular, as opposed to a one-size-fits-all approach. The recommendation, "This product is best for *you*" only makes sense when your advisor actually understands you. The grass may be greener on the other side, but if you prefer strawberry fields you won't be satisfied.

Any financial advisor can offer you a better return. "I can get you 8%, and that's better than your 7%." Sure, 8 is bigger than 7. No one is going to argue that. But at some point, the bottom is going to fall out of the stock market again. How will that impact you? Tax law will change. How will that impact you? Your expenses and cost of living are going to increase. How will that impact you?

The point is simple: the advisor needs to have a genuine interest in who you are. One size doesn't fit all. Earlier today I met with two prospective clients, a husband and wife. They both have Social Security, and he has a pension while she does not. My approach with them is different from my approach with a couple who both possess pensions. They're going to have different needs. Your advisor likewise should attend to your specific needs.

#2. Communication

What type of communication do you expect to receive from your advisor? How frequently do you expect him to communicate with you?

One man's basic service is another man's over-communication. It's all in the eye of the beholder. For this reason, you need to make expectations clear before establishing a business relationship. Ask, "How often should I plan on hearing from you? What are your levels of communication?"

Maybe the answer is, "I'm going to call you once a year, and we'll sit down together annually." Then you're only going to expect one call each year. Maybe the answer is, "I'm very hands-on. You'll hear from me once a month." In that case, if six months roll by and you haven't heard from the advisor, your expectation is not being met.

So many people tell me, "I called my advisor four times. He never returned my call." Or, "I had concerns about my account, so I called my advisor and left a voicemail. I just got an email back saying, 'You're all set.'" Maybe that's how the advisor does business, but the client wasn't comfortable with that. This is your money the advisor is dealing with. You own the ship, so pick a reliable captain who will steer you in the right direction.

In the advisor's defense, no news may be good news. They might be managing your account well. You can give them the benefit of the doubt. But no news might be terrible news. The advisor should be willing to give you enough time to alleviate your worries. If not, it's time to find a new advisor.

Another aspect of communication is access. How much access do you have to the main advisor? With whom else from the advisor's office will you be working? For example, in my office you will hear from four or five different people during the course of our relationship. They have different jobs, roles, and tasks, but they are all here to work for you.

I'm involved in all significant decisions, and my staff handles the details. For example, if you want to process a withdrawal, I'll look it over to make sure it's the right thing to do. Then my staff will process the paperwork and make the withdrawal happen. This is a matter of expectations. I tell all my clients, "When you need something, I'm going to review it. I'll call you and confirm. Then somebody else is going to process the paperwork and follow up."

Setting expectations up front is important because it avoids frustration later. The fear of the unknown creeps in otherwise: "Are they handling it? Are they not? Do I need to be doing something?" Doubt enters and you cannot stop worrying. So have the conversation and set expectations about communication.

#3. Asset Growth

Asset growth might seem straightforward: more is better. But that's not always the case. Let's say your goal is maximizing after-tax income. Your advisor works hard to grow your assets, and they increase 7% in one year. But the IRS changes the tax law, and because your assets are all qualified you now owe 10% more in taxes. Where has that asset growth gotten you now? Not far. If your expectation is after-tax income, and your advisor focuses on pre-tax asset growth, there's a disconnect.

At my seminars, I often ask the crowd, "What do you want your money to do?" The unanimous response is, "Grow!" We all want our money to grow. But what are you willing to sacrifice for that growth? Taking on additional risk may not be worth it.

The fundamental consideration with your assets is, "What rate of return do I need to accomplish my income goals?" Imagine you need a 5% return for long-term sustainability. Your assets should be positioned for that 5% return—not 8%. Even if your advisor thinks he can get you 8% by taking on a bit more risk, why would you do that? You don't need it, and you could lose more money. The greed factor tempts you to take on unnecessary risk in the hope of an unnecessary gain.

The corollary is that you must be satisfied with a smaller return. What if that 8% asset you didn't buy actually does return 8%? Now you are stuck with the 5% return. Will you get mad? Will you want to switch all your money over to the 8% asset? Contentment with what you need will take you a long way in avoiding unnecessary risk.

Even if your assets grow, they may not grow in a way that's right for you. Your advisor offers you a new product with phenomenal growth— but that growth doesn't begin until Year 5, and you need income now. Or vice versa: an income fund will start paying you now, but you really need the money two years down the road. You and your advisor need to direct your income toward the goals that are right for you.

Every year at your annual review, ensure you are still on the right track. You may be comfortable, but don't let up. Keep your foot on the gas pedal. Keep the speed—just because you've been with somebody eight years doesn't mean the ninth year is going to be the same.

What does your advisor talk about during annual reviews? Chasing returns or guaranteeing income? Lots of financial advisors chase returns: "We made 5% here, and we're going to move that money to the 6% asset for next year." But this is a chase you can never complete. You never "catch" your target! If an Olympic race had no visible finish line, the runners would never know where to stop. And if your financial race has no defined finish line, you'll never know when to take your chips off the table and secure your winnings.

An Olympic race features the same finish line for everyone. But in advising, the finish line is unique to you. You need a certain level of income, which may be more or less than the advisor's other clients. Does he know what income you need?

Lots of advisors can get you to X% of returns. Fewer listen to you enough to know what number that "X" should actually be.

#4. Longevity

You might live to 100. Will your money last as long as you do?

Most financial advisors don't really have an age in mind. Maybe they're planning as though you'll live to 85 or 90. Perhaps they use the average life expectancy, without taking into account your particular situation. This is why personalization is crucial. Not everyone has average health, or average family history, or average longevity. You are unique and deserve to be treated as such. Your financial advisor should dig deep to understand who you are, from your grandparents' lifespans to your own eating plans.

Ask the Hard Questions

Maybe you like to think the best of everyone. That's good. But don't let an instinctive trust of others lead you to entrust your money to someone without due diligence.

I recommend that anyone considering a financial advisor ask hard negative questions. Otherwise you may find yourself stuck in a business relationship you're no longer satisfied with. These questions reveal how the advisor will act in bad times, as well as good. If they've laid out a plan for you, will they stick to it? Do they really believe in it? Sometimes prospective clients meet with me, then take my recommendations back to their current advisor. Even though my recommendations differ substantially from his, the advisor often responds, "I can do that instead. Why don't you stick with me?" Out of a sense of faith, longevity, and loyalty, sometimes the client does just that. I laugh a little, because I know they'll be back in two or three years. Their advisor is not delivering, and that's not going to change.

Here are two of my favorite hard questions:

- "Why do clients leave your firm?"
- "What's the most amount of money you've lost for a client? Why?"

The answers to these questions are important. But perhaps even more important is the way they're answered. Does the advisor stay cool under pressure? Is he defensive? Does he shift blame onto the client? "Oh, clients leave my firm because they just didn't like me/the plan/whatever," is not a good answer. That demonstrates a lack of responsibility. You can really learn a lot about a person from how they answer hard questions.

Yes, this is awkward. But better awkward now than later when you've lost 40%—and the advisor is okay with it, and you're not!

Conclusion

You've reached the very last part of the book. Congratulations! As I think back over all the material we've covered, here are three things I hope you remember most.

First, you won't slow down in retirement. Your busy, exciting life is not going to change into stagnation. If anything, you'll engage in even more of what you love to do.

Next, surround yourself with people you believe in and trust. Find people who have your best interests at heart, who point you in the right direction, and who will stay with you along the entire journey. Then keep them close.

Finally, enjoy yourself. The day you retire is the finish line—now it's time for your victory lap. The day you retire is like summiting a mountain—now plant your flag and relish the view. Then climb down the other side at your own pace, breathing the fresh mountain air. The last thing you want to do is have to climb back up to the top. And if you make sure your finances are planned well, you won't have to. You can simply enjoy the descent.

If you want to continue learning about retirement, visit my website at www.FoguthFinancial.com. We offer a free helpful retirement kit, including PDF guides and an educational video series.

Everyone who has made it this far, I appreciate you taking the time to read this book. Questions? I'm happy to give you a personalized answer. If you want to know more about anything in this book, reach out to me using the contact information below. Nothing in financial planning is one-size-fits-all. There's no magic potion. You need a personalized consultation. Know that anytime you want, I'm happy to sit down and have a conversation with you.

Michael Foguth
Michael@FoguthFinancial.com
810-522-5650 | 866-845-4149

Who is Michael?

Michael Foguth guides his clients through the retirement planning process with custom-tailored plans designed to withstand whatever the road ahead may hold. Raised in Mid-Michigan by his parents Michael and Marie, he was taught that faith and family are the foundation to a successful journey through life.

Family is of the utmost importance to Michael; his father being one of 13 and his mother one of 6 instilled the importance of strong family bonds. Michael and his wife Brooke support this belief with the five children they have together. Family is what drives Michael to continue his passion in the retirement planning arena.

Having seen firsthand what improper preparation and market volatility can do to one's retirement, he makes it a point to educate others on what they can do to ensure history does not repeat itself.

Michael's passion led him to specialize in working with retirees and those nearing retirement who desire to protect their hard-earned money and ensure that it is there when they need it. Michael and his team at Foguth Financial Group pride themselves on the long-lasting relationships they have developed with their clients and their families. Not only has he guided his own clients, but also he has trained financial advisors across the country on exactly how to properly plan a successful retirement for their clients. Michael's clientele turns to him when faced with tough decisions that come up during pre- and post-retirement journeys.

Michael is a graduate of Central Michigan University. He was nominated for "Elite 40 under 40" by L. Brooks Patterson in 2014. He has been quoted in Newsweek, The Wall Street Journal, USA Today, TIME Magazine, Yahoo Finance, and Forbes; as well as featured on NBC, ABC, CBS, CNBC, MSNBC, FOX, and FOX Business.

Educating today's retirees plays a key role in the planning that Michael does; he is an educator for the Richness of Life Institute through Central Michigan University and Cleary College.

Michael has become one of the national premier experts when it comes to retirement planning in today's economic times. His first book *Successonomics* was released in September of 2014; the book was co-authored with Steve Forbes. Within its first week it was on five different Amazon best seller lists. His second book, *What You Don't Know About Retirement Income Can Hurt You*, was published in February 2016.

When he is not at work you can find him coaching his children in whatever activity they are playing. The Foguth family is very active within the community. They participate with local and national ordinations such as LOVE INC., A.L.S. of Michigan, Make-A-Wish Foundation, and Relay for Life. Michael and his family are members of 2:42 Church of Brighton.

Michael's broker check information can be found at www.BrokerCheck.Finra.org.

You can connect with Michael by emailing him at Michael@FoguthFinancial.com, connecting with him on Twitter @FoguthFinancial, or going to his Facebook page @FoguthFinancialGroup.

Retirement Spotlight

Authored by Michael Foguth
Editorial Consultant: Caleb DeLon

Michael Foguth

810-522-5650 | 866-845-4149

FoguthFinancial.com
Michael@FoguthFinancial.com

315 W. North St. Suite C
Brighton, MI 48116

ISBN-10: 1-9462-0303-3
ISBN-13: 978-1-946203-03-8

—Disclaimer—

www.ExpertPress.net

Made in the USA
Lexington, KY
07 February 2017